ABOUT THE BOOK

Thoughts on the Origin and Evolution of Evil is a book about the beginnings and outworking of evil. We explore this from the perspective of the Bible. We consider what it might have looked like when Satan fell from glory, which resulted in the origin of evil. We consider the outworking of evil as revealed in the Bible and experienced in life. We include in this analysis the fall of mankind and the ways in which Satan exercises his influence on people. We also consider God's triumph over evil through the cross and resurrection of Jesus Christ.

ACKNOWLEDGEMENTS

I would like to thank my wife, Sara, for her help reviewing this book. I would also like to thank my friends David and Ron for their helpful reviews and valuable insights and suggestions. Above all, I thank the Lord Jesus, whose grace in my life is the ultimate reason I wrote this book. May sinners come to know Him, may He be glorified, and may His Church be strengthened in some small way by this book.

Soli Deo Gloria

ABOUT THE AUTHOR

Scott Leone is an ordained minister with a Master of Divinity degree. He also possesses a bachelor's and master's degree in aeronautical engineering. He is married to his wife, Sara, and they have three grown children. Scott works as an engineer, but he has served in various pastoral roles and been involved in church planting.

THOUGHTS ON THE ORIGIN AND EVOLUTION OF EVIL

A Christian's Perspective

THOUGHTS ON THE ORIGIN AND EVOLUTION OF EVIL

A Christian's Perspective

Scott Leone

EQUIP PRESS

Colorado Springs

THOUGHTS ON THE ORIGIN
AND EVOLUTION OF EVIL

Copyright © 2020 and Scott Leone

All rights reserved. No part of this publication may be reproduced, distributed, or transmitted in any form or by any means, without prior written permission.

Published by Equip Press, Colorado Springs, CO

Unless otherwise noted, all Scripture quotations are taken from the Christian Standard Bible® Copyright © 2017 by Holman Bible Publishers. Used by permission. Christian Standard Bible®, and CSB® are federally registered trademarks of Holman Bible Publishers.

First Edition: 2020
Thoughts on the Origin And Evolution of Evil / Scott Leone
Paperback ISBN: 978-1-951304-44-7
eBook ISBN: 978-1-951304-45-4

CONTENTS

About the Book	1
Acknowledgements	3
About the Author	5
Introduction	13

Part I *The Origin of Evil*	**15**
1. The Eternal God	17
2. His Glorious Creation	21
3. Angels Fall	23
4. Reproofs Ignored	25
5. Unrestrained Evil	27
6. Castaways	29
7. Lying Presumption	31
8. False Judgment	33
9. Willful Abuse	35
10. God's Wisdom Revealed	37
11. Satan's Temptation	39
12. A Direct Challenge to God	41
13. A Murderer from the Beginning	43
14. Demonic Paranoia	45
15. A Kindred Spirit	47

Part II *The Evolution of Evil*	**49**
16. Interlude – God's Promises	51
17. Growth in Evil	53
18. Pattern Recognition	55

19.	The Temptation of Power	57
20.	Chaos	59
21.	Fiery Arrows	61
22.	Direct Assault	63
23.	Mind Games	65
24.	False Promises	67
25.	Cloaking	69
26.	The Deception of Autonomy	71
27.	Violence as a Means to an End	73
28.	Evil Alliances	75
29.	Deceitful Manipulations	77
30.	Satan's Goal	79
31.	Satan's Impact	81
32.	Satan's Image	83
33.	The Devil Made Me Do It	85
34.	Blame it on the Devil	87

Part III *God's Response to Evil* — **89**

35.	Seeing as God Sees	91
36.	Recovering Reality	93
37.	Divine Remedy	95
38.	God's Triumph	99
39.	God's Heart	101

INTRODUCTION

*"But the Lord is faithful;
he will strengthen you and guard you from the evil one."*

(2 Thessalonians 3:3)

Life is not about politics or personalities—it's about God. That truth is hard for some people to accept. People can become very used to and skilled at seeing the world without any reference to God. God seems irrelevant. Life goes on. Days begin and end, and history continues.

But there are hidden realities that it takes faith to "see."[1] God is one such reality—the Ultimate Reality. Another reality are angels—as is the existence of heaven and hell. To become content, living without considering these realities is not wise and can only end in ruin.

Convincing people of such realities is a struggle, but one worth engaging in. As a Christian, I value my soul and the souls of others. I want to do everything I can to help fellow sinners see God's light and rightly understand His universe. To that end, I present this book.

This book expresses some ideas that cannot be validated by direct revelation from God in the Bible. I understand that, so I

---

1   Hebrews 11:1.

present them as *derived* from the Bible and from biblical ideas.[2] The absolute and historical accuracy of some things presented here are unknown. Therefore, take them as theories and subject them to the test of God's Providence (if that's possible).[3]

Nevertheless, there is no question in this author's mind that much of what is presented here is accurate and true. There are principles and strategies of evil that cannot be denied and are evident by both Scripture and experience. It is my hope that the reader will be challenged and helped by this book.

Although the devil is not a being to be taken lightly, he is also not to be looked for "behind every tree" or "under every rock," so to speak. The problem with a book like this is that it might lead to an unreasonable view of life and current events.

On the other hand, the problem most of us have is that we do not take the devil seriously enough. In that regard, I hope this book will help people become aware of the true enemy.

The goal of this book is not to make the reader become overly focused on Satan, but to move the reader to prayer, a trust in God, and a desire to believe and proclaim the gospel of His Son, Jesus Christ.[4]

---

[2] The method used here to *derive* conclusions from the Bible might be called extrapolative deduction. In the same way one might deduce what it is like in heaven based on revelation in the Bible about the Fruit of the Spirit, one might deduce what evil resulted from based on the revelation of evil in the Bible and ensuing experience. Granted, such extrapolations are speculative. The author admits that such speculations can take on dogmatic overtones. But it is my desire to be reasonable and not novel, so that such speculations result in possible explanations rather than stated facts. The reader is asked to keep this in mind.

[3] 1 Corinthians 4:5.

[4] We ask God in the Lord's Prayer, "deliver us from evil." That includes being delivered from the evil one, Satan, and all his schemes.

PART I

THE ORIGIN OF EVIL

We begin with some thoughts on how evil may have begun. What was heaven like and how did holy angels fall from innocence to a state of unmitigated evil?

1

THE ETERNAL GOD

"Before the mountains were born, before you gave birth to the earth and the world, from eternity to eternity, you are God."

Psalm 90:2

Not much is known of ancient heaven and its glory before the earth was made and mankind created. We can only speculate what might have taken place based upon the revelation contained in the Bible.

We know the character of God. He is love; He embodies joy, peace, patience, kindness, goodness, gentleness, faithfulness, self-control, and much more. For our purposes, we focus upon His gentleness.

Gentleness is akin to humility. God's humility is seen by His great restraint of infinite power and by the gentleness with which He conducts Himself. Power under control, infinite power, restrained by divine gentleness—that's God.

His wisdom and understanding are infinite. He sees far beyond the moment, peering into eternity in ways that are incomprehensible to mere creatures.[5]

---

5   Isaiah 55:8-9.

His glory enfolds His entire being. His character is holy, without any moral blemish or hint of evil. His nature defines holiness, righteousness, and truth. He is the fount of all that is. He is self-existent, without beginning or end, eternal, unchangeable, and independent of all He made. He is God.[6]

He exists in three persons: the Father, the Son, and the Holy Spirit. This tri-unity of God is a mystery to us. One God, truly united and existing in three persons. He is never alone and always content—yet the Godhead chose to create.

Why a creation? It was for His glory.[7] The Father will be glorified by His wisdom, sovereignty, and love in creation; the Son by His instrumentality in bringing it about and His divine hand in holding it together; the Spirit by His power in carrying out all that was needed to bring something out of nothing.

Who can fully understand the greatness of God? Who can comprehend the depth of His wisdom and power? Nothing can compare to the One who made everything. There is no measure or standard to which we can compare God, since He is greater than all He made.[8]

Therefore, it is hard to imagine what heaven was like in ancient times when holy angels dwelt before Him and sin and rebellion were unknown. But such a time did exist. For God makes all things good.[9] His original creation stands holy and without blame before Him; it can be no other way. Would God create rebellion against Himself? No. That's not His nature.[10]

---

6   Psalm 90:1-2.

7   Psalm 8.

8   Isaiah 40:25-25; 55:8.

9   Genesis 1:31.

10   Habakkuk 1:13.

So, what happened back in ancient glory? How did holy angels dwelling before a holy God become unholy? There is a mystery here. But the key to understanding this seems to be the idea of instability.[11] God made creatures holy and blameless before Him, but He required of them their constant love, trust, and devotion. Yet, a fundamental instability existed by which some fell from innocence, while others held on to stand firm in glory.

Why God allowed such instability we do not know. But it was His will, so we can trust Him. Perhaps, in His infinite wisdom, this was the only way He could create and maintain ultimate stability. Perhaps the juxtaposition of His love and His wrath were required for an "even keel" into eternity. Perhaps this was how He could reveal His grace and mercy to His creation. We can only speculate here. But we can definitely say God's reasons resulted in His own glory and in all He made, giving ultimate honor to Him.[12]

---

11   Ecclesiastes 7:29 may express that idea in mankind's instability.

12   Isaiah 45:23.

THOUGHTS ON THE ORIGIN AND EVOLUTION OF EVIL

2

HIS GLORIOUS CREATION

"In the beginning God created the heavens and the earth."

(Genesis 1:1)

To describe heaven's creatures is to enter a great unknown. Only what is revealed in Scripture exposes the hidden secrets of these glorious beings. Yet, their glory is but a mere reflection of God's glory. Like the moon reflects the sun's light, so the creature reflects the Creator's glory—but it is not the source of the glory.

For the creature to emanate such glory not its own must present unusual experiences, even temptations. Creatures make comparisons with other creatures. Creatures are learning and processing knowledge as it is gained. What the creature does with such knowledge can determine a course of life.

We do not know what specifically began to possess the mind of one particularly glorious angelic being, named Satan.[13] We can

---

13   Satan is among the many names given to the devil in the Bible. Revelation 12:9.

only imagine what might have led to his fall from glory and the fall with him of many others.

But we must keep in mind their original glory. All that God first created was glorious and wonderful. How they must have first appeared before God in glory! How they shone! How they began to speak and interact!

Power and ability began to be used and tested. Not all creatures had the same abilities. They differed in wisdom, understanding, and power. The strongest began to feel their strength. Conversely, the weakest felt their weaknesses. Those with sharper understanding excelled more quickly than those with lesser. However, all was still harmonious and happy.

None would yet think to use their glory for their own selfish purposes. But alas, we can conceive the possibility that great power brought with it a kind of temptation. The inclination to overstep was present. Like a stone placed precariously at the top of a hill, all it takes is a certain nudge to send it over. All it took was a certain choice made to nudge an otherwise holy being over the edge to misuse its power and glory.

3

ANGELS FALL

"Everyone with a proud heart is detestable to the Lord; be assured, he will not go unpunished."

(Proverbs 16:5)

We do not know the exact process that led to holy angels falling from their glory and innocence.[14] But we may speculate based upon the revelation of their glory and their present state with all its deceitful features.[15]

As knowledge grows, presumption can grow alongside it. To presume is to assume more than our knowledge justifies. Presumption is essentially an unwarranted extrapolation of knowledge. Bits of truth are forwarded in the mind to predict an

---

14 However, examine the language of Ezekiel 28:1-19. The descriptions of the King of Tyre may very well be allusions to what happened with Satan when he fell. See also Jude 1:6.

15 Here we use "extrapolative deduction," taking what we presently know from Scripture and deduce a possible scenario that led to this condition.

outcome. Left unchecked by facts, such extrapolations can produce a false or imaginative view of reality.

Initially, presumption can be harmless. Fact checking can remove presumption and keep it in line. But unchecked, presumption produces false judgment. Then, one begins to think wrongly of others. Judgments that are false can never produce righteousness. Yet, as with presumption, even false judgments can be corrected by good information. One need not commit sin by either presumption or false judgment if one seeks the proper corrective knowledge. Like temptation itself, these are not sinful unless they are taken to the next level.

Alas, here is where one's glory and power can push one over the edge and down the hill to a complete fall.[16] Glory can blind one when he forgets that God alone is the source of that glory. Humility becomes harder when we begin to focus on our own eminent glory.

That last step following presumption and false judgment is abuse and domination. Here, power becomes an end in itself. The will becomes all important. Presumption blinds, while false judgment builds it up to the point when finally abuse and domination result.

The fall from God's gentleness and restraint is now complete. The creature has left his Creator and has begun to exercise attributes not given him by God. Sadly, for such fallen angelic beings, there is no way back up the hill to innocence.[17]

---

[16] Proverbs 16:18, "Pride comes before destruction, and an arrogant spirit before a fall."

[17] See also Proverbs 11:2, 18:12, 29:23.

4

REPROOFS IGNORED

"Because they hated knowledge, didn't choose to fear the Lord, were not interested in my counsel, and rejected all my correction, they will eat the fruit of their way and be glutted with their own schemes."

(Proverbs 1:29-31)

One wonders, at the start of Satan's folly in exalting himself, if God didn't warn or reprove him in some way. It certainly is in God's nature to do that.[18] So, let's speculate for a moment that He did. What might the reproof have looked like?

God's reproofs are gentle and direct, yet sometimes can also be subtle.[19] It is His kind nature to be gentle and patient. Yet, after His warning and the repeated ignoring of it, God will pronounce

---

18 Furthermore, Romans 5:13 reminds us that where there is no law there is no sin. So, one could assume God did warn Satan, thus establishing his sin upon his ignoring of God's warning.

19 Consider God's words to Cain in Genesis 4:7 for an example of His subtle manner of warning.

judgment.[20] His judgments are final. There is no court of appeals.[21]

As God warned Adam and Eve, He may also have warned Satan and those following Satan's leadership. With Adam and Eve, God directly spelled out the consequences of certain behavior before they committed the act of such behavior—with no way to undo it. God warned Adam and Eve that if they ate of a certain tree's fruit that they would die. So, if God warned Satan, what might God have said?

Perhaps God warned Satan that His present course of behavior is taking him in a direction that is at odds with God's revealed will for him. Perhaps God warned that his course would turn him against God. Perhaps God warned him that disappointment would result if he were to exalt himself above the place that God had put him.

The point is, however, that if such warnings took place, Satan ignored them. He continued past the point of no return and only gained momentum in his folly. The result was permanent damage to himself and angelic beings who followed him, and a fixed state of rebellion that will only end in eternal condemnation.

Furthermore, we can add that however the angelic fall happened, Satan has no one to blame but himself. He is completely responsible for his behavior, as are those angelic beings who followed him.

---

20   Proverbs 29:1.

21   Jude 1:6.

5

UNRESTRAINED EVIL

"He must not be a new convert, or he might become conceited and incur the same condemnation as the devil."

(1 Timothy 3:6)

What was God doing or thinking while some angelic beings began down the slippery slope to their eventual doom? We do not know. But we do know God was patient; He was long-suffering.[22]

Perhaps God waited to see how His creatures would respond to the entrance of a disturbing force of will, which caused many to wonder what was happening. One gets the idea that God knew those who would resist this will to power and those who would join it.

Consider the following.

As the power of a domineering spirit grew in a few, others who reflected upon the good character of their Creator, sensed something wrong and held themselves back. They refused to join the rebellion that was forming, even if they didn't fully understand

---

22 Compare this patience to Romans 3:25.

it yet. Their heart remained devoted to God. They knew their glory reflected God's, so they restrained themselves in godly humility, awaiting their Lord's judgment rather than passing their own.

But the crowds grew around Satan—the one with the newfound power. How he spoke, how he led, and how he promised! No one else had sounded quite like him before. This was new. God said nothing, or at least did nothing, giving them the false impression of approval.

Oh, how the falling army of angels misread the gentleness and patience of God! How they presumed upon His kindness, falsely judged His anger as imaginary, and abused their limited authority before the divine King.

From such a scenario, we deduce that evil was the gradual fall from glory of the creature to the place of arrogance. The creature slowly felt he could replace the Creator.

Other angels were appalled.

God suffered long, then spoke.

The true Judge pronounced their doom. They had allowed their own glory to rob God of His glory. God will never tolerate that from His creatures.[23] To rob God of what rightly belongs to Him alone is the essence of evil. Their conceit resulted in their condemnation![24]

Having fallen from innocence, these angelic beings became unrestrained in their evil.

---

23 Isaiah 42:8.

24 The progression of events given here is presented as a possibility, not as historical fact, since we are not given such information in Scripture. This is illustrative of how one can fall spiritually.

6

CASTAWAYS

"Yet when Michael the archangel was disputing with the devil in an argument about Moses's body, he did not dare utter a slanderous condemnation against him but said, 'The Lord rebuke you!'"

(Jude 1:9)

What happened next is also a mystery. God created the earth and universe, and it seems Scripture alludes that the fallen angels were banished there to await their final judgment. They became castaways.

Driven from the direct presence of God's glory, these fallen angels had nothing left to restrain them but God's divine or angelic intervention and rebuke.[25] They became emboldened in their newfound realm. God's wrath was executed swiftly but not finally.[26] They knew another day was coming wherein their removal from God's creation would consign them to an abyss from which they would never escape.

---

25 In other words, only God or angels of equal power can restrain fallen angels.

26 2 Peter 2:4.

In the mystery of angelic beings, these castaways can still manage to have great influence upon God's earthly creation. How can they do it? All we know is they can do it, yet in a limited way as God constrains them.[27]

These fallen beings are not infinite in power or presence. They are powerful and capable, but they do have limitations. Their malice seems unbounded, as they have come to despise all that represents God.

Beings that fall from humility can only exalt themselves. Their will is to prop themselves up, gratify themselves, and have no other rule or law to manage them. Only rebuke can hold their selfish will in check. Even Michael, the archangel, called on God to rebuke Satan.[28]

This is the lot of a fallen creature. The will becomes unrestrained in its selfish desires. God and God's laws mean nothing. No foothold exists to constrain the evil passions of a presumptuous being misled by its own glory and full of its own power in the exercise of its will. In such a state, the being becomes intoxicated by itself and must seek its own justification at every turn to keep the illusion of power and glory going.

These castaways have lost all touch with God and the holy angels. Nothing but conflict remains.

---

27   God's constraint is presented in 2 Thessalonians 2:6-7.

28   And, in Revelation 12 we read of Michael battling and overcoming Satan.

7

LYING PRESUMPTION

*"But the prophet who presumes to speak a message in my name
that I have not commanded him to speak, or who speaks
in the name of other gods—that prophet must die."*

(Deuteronomy 18:20)

To presume something is true when it is not is to accept a lie. Any creature, angelic or human, can presume something. But those who seek correct knowledge never allow presumption to become something worse. The creature that continues with a false presumption is the one who becomes deceived by its lie.

Presumption presents a false case. It paints a false picture and misrepresents reality. Therefore, presumption is a means of perpetuating falsehood unless corrected.

One can only imagine what fallen angels began to believe about God or the holy angels who did not agree with them. Perhaps they began to see weakness in them. Yes, they may have thought they saw God as weak for not fulfilling their own ideas.

Presumption fills one with a high view of self. Presumption puffs up self while looking down on others, even God. Presumption creates a false reality. Yet, the mind fully engaged by presumptuous lies fails to see its own blindness.

Like seeing the world through colored glasses, presumption misrepresents reality. Can you imagine where a being can be led who follows presumption?

Even when elements of presumption are corrected, since a fallen being is given over to its lies, it can never accept that correction. Only rebuke can redirect the presumptuous spirit, but even then, it is only a grudging movement it makes.

A presumptuous mind never humbles itself, never sees its true error, and never leaves the path of lies. This is because it accepts false ideas of God and falls short of truly knowing Him, loving Him, honoring Him, or being devoted to Him.

The presumptuous being is always led astray. Whatever fervor it appears to produce for God, it is misled and designed to give the creature itself the ultimate glory.

8

FALSE JUDGMENT

"So don't judge anything prematurely, before the Lord comes, who will both bring to light what is hidden in darkness and reveal the intentions of the hearts. And then praise will come to each one from God."

(1 Corinthians 4:5)

When a lie begins to take root, the result can only be false discernment. Lies lead to wrong judgments of others. Like false witnesses in a court of law, injustice results and the innocent are painted as guilty, the kind as wicked, and the righteous as unholy.

False judgment follows presumption and turns right into wrong and wrong into right in our thinking. The mind loses its ability to decide right from wrong. The deceived being is left justifying its own beliefs without any means of redirection.[29]

Once again, only rebuke can shift the mind that is clinging to falsehood. Yet, it still maintains its correctness even through

---

29 Reflect upon Romans 1:28-32.

the rebuke. Nothing seems to change, the mind gripped by lies.[30]

Fallen angels know a great deal. They have seen and experienced more than humans can even imagine. Yet, they remain unchanged. Their mind continually faces reality, looking for ways to promote and justify self. Because God's glory is not truly their desire, but rather their own glory, their mind cannot move from the lies that give justification and power to them.

Like a drunken person, the mind so governed by falsehood. Falsehood intoxicates. There is a feeling of power. Humility is seen as weakness, and self is exalted. Falsehood is perpetuated for the being's own satisfaction.

Lies beget more lies. Falsehood leads the spirit further and further from God and reality. The result is deception, and the spirit can no longer be trusted at any level, for the machinations of their mind are always to derive a self-fulfilling scheme that makes them feel good about themselves.

What a desperate state is a mind led astray from God by falsehood and lies![31] Who can tell what it will do next? Who knows where it will end up? Who can quantify the damage it will create?

---

30   Proverbs 27:22.

31   Isaiah 5:20, and the broader context of that verse.

9

WILLFUL ABUSE

"But if you have bitter envy and selfish ambition in your heart, don't boast and deny the truth. Such wisdom does not come down from above but is earthly, unspiritual, demonic."

—➤➤⋘←—

(James 3:14-15)

The only result of being lost in presumption and false judgment is willful abuse and domination. Restraints governed by a right relationship to God are not there. Rebuke only temporarily alters direction. The will becomes the driving force to steer the spirit.

Imagine a rudderless ship being driven by changing winds. So is the being driven by circumstances, because there is no true connection to God to steer their course aright. Faith and trust in God do not truly exist in them. The being rests upon its own will, not God's. Self-trust replaces humble trust in God's goodness and will.

There can be but one result for such a being—abuse and a perpetual desire to dominate. It can never subordinate, except under the power of a stronger will. But then it is only a grudging subordination—one that is quickly abandoned when opportunity presents itself.

Abuse dominates the will of others to gain a false sense of power and rightness. Exercising dominance helps create the illusion of one's own glory. It becomes a justifying power that must be exercised in increasingly more clever and manipulative ways so that it feels it cannot possibly lose.

Rebukes are mere temporary setbacks to the abusive and domineering spirit. Humility is not there, at least not genuine humility. False deference may exist, but only to deflect criticism or buy time for a new strategy of dominance.

How impossible it is to deal with such a being! Only God can master its meanderings or curb its power.

Imagine the force that fallen angels have become. Their will is everything to them. No amount of deception is too small for them to exercise so they can gratify their own will and exalt their own false glory.[32]

---

[32] See how the Man of Lawlessness is led by Satan to proclaim himself God in 2 Thessalonians 2:4. See how demons hide behind idols to receive worship in 1 Corinthians 10:20.

10

GOD'S WISDOM REVEALED

*"The Lord founded the earth by wisdom
and established the heavens by understanding."*

—⇒≫≪⇐—

(Proverbs 3:19)

One may ask, "Why didn't God stop these fallen angels or condemn them immediately?" Once again, we do not know the full answer, at least not yet. However, God's actions display His wisdom, which in part gives us the answer. God created mankind.

Human beings were made of something less firm than angels. Angels seem to possess immortal bodies, which are not subject to death or decay. But God made beings far weaker and far more fragile in nature. Why?

It would seem God did this to ultimately reveal His glory and wisdom in how He created all things. It would seem He did it to bring ultimate order to His creation by revealing His grace and His justice through this creation.[33]

---

33 Ephesians 2:7; 3:10. Holy angels learned about God's wrath, having seen poured out on Satan and the fallen angels, but they learn about the depth of His grace as it's poured out on the Church.

No longer would there be a question in any being's mind about God's nature. Neither God's gentleness nor His wrath could ever be challenged once God revealed Himself and His plans through the weaknesses of human nature.

As was mentioned above, there is no revelation in the Bible that holy angels were given a test of obedience by God. But God did give such a direct test to mankind. The first man and woman were given freedom to eat of all the trees in God's garden, except for one. Eating from the forbidden tree would result in death.[34]

The Creator had every right to demand such specific obedience. But the presence of the test gave the primary fallen angel, Satan, a temptation to abuse power and assert his will that he could not resist.

Did God know Satan would try this? Surely, He did. For it will be through mankind that God will completely defeat Satan and thoroughly reveal His great gentleness, grace, and love. Even the holy angels will marvel and be emboldened to defend heaven once they understand God's great plans.[35]

The wise Creator is never diverted from His plans by evil. For His will cannot fail nor be thwarted by mere creatures, nor will He ultimately allow His glory to be stolen or trampled upon.[36]

---

[34] See Genesis 2.

[35] This will be demonstrated below.

[36] Isaiah 42:8; 55:11.

11

SATAN'S TEMPTATION

"And the Lord God commanded the man, 'You are free to eat from any tree of the garden, but you must not eat from the tree of the knowledge of good and evil, for on the day you eat from it, you will certainly die.'"

(Genesis 2:16-17)

When we think of Adam and Eve in the Garden of Eden, we think of innocence led astray by Satan's tempting them to disobey God. Yet, wasn't God's command not to eat of a certain tree only a temptation for Satan? It presented no temptation to Adam and Eve, who easily contented themselves with each other and everything else God had provided.

The command not to eat of a certain tree tempted Satan to assert his will and display his dominance. How could he resist the chance to ruin God's latest creation? How could this presumptuous, self-justifying fallen creature not seize upon the opportunity to besmirch God's character and justify his own false view of reality?

So, Satan used his unusual powers to speak to Eve through a creature: a snake. Yes, fallen angels have unusual powers that have, at times throughout history, been allowed by God to act unrestrained. In the Bible, the book of Revelation highlights Satan's unusual, apparent supernatural powers to perform signs and wonders. Both Jesus Christ and the apostle Paul also spoke about those powers, as recorded in the Bible.[37] So is it any wonder that Satan speaks through a snake?

The tempter was tempted. He gave into the temptation to abuse his power, and he became the tempter first to Eve and then through her to Adam.

What was Satan thinking here? Why did he do it? Was it spite? Was it mere malice? Was it self-justification of will? Was it to prop up his false view of reality to feel better about himself and what he had done in former times? Was it a convoluted attempt to prove to God that he was right, and God was wrong? We don't know.

But key to this event was that Satan never inquired of God nor acted in love or respect for what God had just created. The battle was on. Satan had declared war on God. It is a futile effort. But arrogance knows no restraint and perpetuates the illusion of a glory that will never materialize.[38]

---

37   Revelation 16:14; 2Thessalonians 2:9; Matthew 24:24.

38   Consider all the vain delusions of glory by dictators and conquerors.

12

A DIRECT CHALLENGE TO GOD

"Now the serpent was the most cunning of all the wild animals that the Lord God had made."

(Genesis 3:1a)

When Satan tempted Eve to disobey God by eating of the one tree God commanded mankind not to eat of, Satan was directly challenging God. The same errors that fed Satan's mind and led to his fall, are the very ones he places before the unwitting mind of innocent Eve.[39]

First, Satan disarms Eve's defenses by presumption. "Has God said?" Satan asks, questioning God's word. Presumption presents something as true when it is not. In this case, it presents a truth as false, when it is not.

This disarms Eve. She had never encountered such a lie before. Yet, to her credit, her initial instinct was to fall back on what God had said.

Therefore, Satan must move to step two, which is false judgment. A lying witness presents a convincing case that becomes

---

39 See Genesis 3 for the full account.

hard to refute. "No! You won't die," said Satan. He bears her witness of a false reality. And she is defenseless against such a witness.

God requires trust and devotion. He wants us to trust His love and goodness and remain implicitly devoted to Him, no matter what is presented to us—especially when what is presented contradicts His word. Eve's faith was too weak and unformed. Indeed, the same fundamental instability found in angels exists in humans. God knew her fall would happen, and He allowed it for a greater purpose.[40]

Feeling he had her on her heels, Satan then moves in for the kill. "You will be like God," he promised her. "You will know good and evil," he said. "Power and will can be yours," Satan was saying, just like they were supposedly now his.

Temptation to self-glory is huge. If it is hard for an angel to be humble against the false promise of success, imagine how hard it was for Eve. She and Adam had just been spun from God's creative hands. Inexperience and ignorance were theirs in their innocence, and Satan exploited it.

Satan could not resist challenging God to cast aspersions on Him and justify his own fatal course of life.

---

40 We deduce that God knew mankind would fall from the eternal wisdom and revealed will of God. Deuteronomy 29:29 reminds us that the secret mysteries of the universe belong to God alone. But we know that "before the foundation of the world" God planned redemption

(Ephesians 1:4). So, this deduction is not unwarranted.

13

A MURDERER FROM THE BEGINNING

"You are of your father the devil, and you want to carry out your father's desires. He was a murderer from the beginning and does not stand in the truth, because there is no truth in him. When he tells a lie, he speaks from his own nature, because he is a liar and the father of lies."

(John 8:44)

To murder is to take away the life of another in an unlawful way. To kill innocent human beings is murder. Satan killed Adam and Eve. For by their disobedience to God, death entered the world.

Death did not immediately take place. Perhaps that surprised Satan. Perhaps Satan initially thought they would perish and leave him alone. Who knows? But in any case, God did not bring death upon them immediately and instead offered a solution. One born of the woman would crush Satan and deliver them from the curse of death.[41]

---

41   Genesis 3:15.

We can imagine that Satan now had his sights on Adam and Eve anew. They had children. Offspring were born to them. A son appeared, named Cain. Then, another son, Abel. What did this mean for Satan? Abel appeared to be the one who loved God. Was Abel that one whom God promised would crush him?

Satan couldn't allow that to happen, so he set out to destroy Abel. It is highly likely that Satan gripped Cain's heart with jealousy and hatred, which tempted him to murder his brother.[42]

We see in Cain's nature the same fallen attributes that Satan possesses. Indeed, those attributes have now become part of human nature since the fall of Adam and Eve. Presumption, false judgment, and abuse to dominate entered mankind as surely as it possessed Satan and the fallen angels.

God's holy image in mankind became tarnished by the same fallen nature that tarnished holy angels. Sin now became the natural course. Self-justification of the will to establish one's own glory also became the driving force.

God urged Cain to resist sin. Cain ignored God's word the same way his mother had, only now he was aided by his own deceitful heart. So Cain murdered Abel.[43] And Satan had his first actual victim of death. Convinced now that his power could dominate humans, more horror was yet to come.

---

[42] Satan's involvement here is an assumption, but consider Acts 5:3-4, where Satan filled a man's heart with lies that led to evil behavior. And consider that John describes Cain as "of the evil one" in 1 John 3:12. If Satan is not credited with direct involvement, he certainly is involved indirectly.

[43] See Genesis 4 for the full account of Cain and Abel.

14

DEMONIC PARANOIA

"Therefore rejoice, you heavens, and you who dwell in them!
Woe to the earth and the sea, because the devil has come down to you
with great fury, because he knows his time is short."

(Revelation 12:12)

It's ironic how seriously Satan takes God's promise of a Savior, a Deliverer who will crush him. I say ironic because people usually don't take God so seriously. Demons do, but they still act contrary to God's will and in support of their own will.

Throughout biblical history, it is recorded how Satan attempted to crush God's anointed one before that one could crush him. Cain slaughtered Abel. Later, Pharaoh will seek to destroy the sons of Israel as Moses was born. Then too, Herod will try to murder God's son, Jesus, while yet a young child.

We may never know the full extent of Satan's paranoia[44] when

---

44 Paranoia assumes an irrational fear. Some of Satan's fears are quite rational as he knows his doom is certain. But sin also produces irrational fears that lead to wicked behavior. King Saul's treatment of David is an example of this. See 1 Samuel 18-31.

it comes to how often he sought to destroy the one he thought might spell his doom. However, God's plans cannot be thwarted. While Satan's malice did not stop God's plan, it did spread pain and suffering to many.

This demonic paranoia accompanies fallen angels, because they know their doom is inevitable. Perhaps then, they look at people and historical events and wonder if God is using them to hasten the day of their destruction.

Irrational fear and paranoia are a result of believing lies and focusing on one's own will and desires. Unmet desire[45] can breed an irrational fear that eventually does things without faith and without true reason. Fear blinds the mind and produces a reaction that is chaotic and anarchistic.

Satan knows that out of chaos he can hope to redirect the course of history to delay God's plans and continue to establish his own. Like smoke in the eyes or a whirling sandstorm, Satan clouds the understanding to force people to react hastily and thus cause further damage, or even destruction, for themselves for failing to act in faith.

Such chaos is the hallmark of many political movements. And sadly, people become Satan's unwitting pawns.

---

[45] Consider the unmitigated "thirst" in fallen angels (a similar thirst exists in fallen people). By thirst I mean spiritual emptiness. There is no access to God's rivers of living water, no internal means to quench desire, no way to fill the void, no rest beside still waters. The Bible often speaks of hell as a place of weeping and gnashing of teeth (e.g. Matthew 8:12; 13:42; 24:51; 25:30).

15

A KINDRED SPIRIT

"Now when it was time for supper, the devil had already put it into the heart of Judas, Simon Iscariot's son, to betray him."

(John 13:2)

Sin in human beings finds a willing ally in Satan, and Satan finds a willing ally in human sin. The two have similar natures when it comes to the deceptive nature of sin. Sin is all that is contrary to God's being and nature. It is the essence of evil and the power behind it.

As presumption forms the basis for a false reality, so Satan finds a friend and willing comrade in mankind by fostering presumptuous lies. A false and lying view of reality is always contrary to God's glory and seeking to establish one's own.

Satan has an easy time questioning God within people, causing doubt, and making God out to be the real problem. Sin enables presumption to take root in people. False reality ensues, and who knows the chaos that can follow?

Satan then uses the tactic of false accusations to foster further discontent and strengthen his own foothold in the human heart. False accusations against God, or about ourselves or others, are all designed to lead us to make false judgments. Acting upon false judgment will anger God[46] and once more produce the chaos that gives Satan delaying power over the progress of godliness—a perceived victory for him.

In the muddy waters of lies, the weakness of the human spirit often yields to abuse and dominance. The defense of self and will become the driving justification for the one consumed in a lying reality. Satan has found a kindred spirit, and he exploits it in every way.

Like Cain, who failed to overcome sin knocking at his door, so people fail to stop the onslaught of falsehood that motivates them to act foolishly and incur God's wrath.

If Satan cannot destroy directly, then he can burn people by pushing them too close to the fire. God is a consuming fire when provoked. Satan knows how to use the will of man to provoke God. And sadly, people are complicit, unaware of the devilish powers driving them ahead to destruction.[47]

---

46 See Psalm 78:17-22 as an example of acting upon false judgments.

47 See the case in Numbers 31:16.

PART II

THE EVOLUTION OF EVIL

We now begin to think about the growth and outworking of evil. How has evil matured, adapted, and developed as observed from Scripture and experience?

16

INTERLUDE – GOD'S PROMISES

*B*efore we dive into the growth and outworking of evil, let us explore some of the great promises of God. He encourages mankind with words of victory over sin through His own plan of redemption.

God's plan began to be revealed, as stated above, immediately after Adam and Eve sinned. God promised a Deliverer to rescue fallen humans and crush Satan. The revelation of that Deliverer, and how God moved history to bring Him about, is truly the greatest story ever told.

Like an oasis in a desert or a patch of beautifully sweet flowers among rocky crags, is the unfolding of God's story of redemption. Let us never think that evil is prevailing. It may win a battle, but ultimate victory is the Lord's. He makes that clear, as the Bible reveals the Lord's triumph through His faithful remnant and His Son.

God wonderfully demonstrates His sovereign and gracious plan through the lineage of people like Adam, Enoch, Noah, Abraham, Isaac, Jacob, whose name is changed to Israel, Judah, King David, and Mary—all the way to the birth of Jesus. These Bible characters and their stories demonstrate that history is truly "His story." Evil is continually frustrated, as God foils the plans of the Evil One and blesses His faithful ones, revealing His love and grace that culminates in His Son appearing.

The story of God's faithfulness to His plan of redemption continues after Jesus' death, resurrection, and ascension through the Church. Initially, we see the Apostles gifted by Christ and inspired by the Holy Spirit with the ability to reveal truths about the gospel of Jesus Christ that illuminates God's redemptive plan, which included all peoples of the earth. The Deliverer promised right after the fall of Adam and Eve will be the Savior of the world.

God's promises include not only a Deliverer, but a resurrection and eternal glory. There will be a new heaven and new earth devoid of sin—only peace, joy, and righteousness. The humble shall truly inherit the earth, a new earth, restored from the ravages of evil.

The Deliverer, Jesus Christ, will also come again. He came the first time for redemption. The next time will be for judgment and the restoration of all things.[48] That will be God's final victory over evil.

Therefore, as we begin to explore the sad outworking of evil, let us keep in mind God's promises so wonderfully revealed in the Bible.

---

[48] Some Christians understand the Bible also to teach that before the Judgment there will be a Millennial Kingdom where Christ reigns.

17

GROWTH IN EVIL

"They became callous and gave themselves over to promiscuity for the practice of every kind of impurity with a desire for more and more."

(Ephesians 4:19)

It's hard to imagine that evil can grow worse, but it can. Evil learns; evil evolves.[49] To know good and evil is to have the capability to grow and evolve in evil. And the good is not pursued to drive out evil, but to perfect evil as a way of life contrary to the good.[50]

There is nothing good in Satan or fallen angels—or fallen people for that matter. That's not to suggest there is no dignity in them, respect due them, or knowledge of good in them. It is to state that the capability to do good without any mixture of sin is not

---

49 Observe the progress of evil in humans. There is a gradual development that humans may not even be aware of. See the account of Hazael in 2 Kings 8.

50 This is the conclusion we come to from Satan's temptation of Eve to know good and evil. Clearly the knowledge of good there is self-serving.

there. All the motions of the will are so intertwined with falsehood and deceit that pure moral goodness is not possible from a fallen state of being.

Mind, emotion, and will are all tarnished by sin and result in movements that mix lies and deceptions and pride and selfishness with all actions and thoughts. God calls even the imaginations of the human mind evil.[51] And if that's true of fallen people, it is doubly true of fallen angels.

Hence, time and experience only serve to enhance and perfect the deceits of sin. The heart's inclinations to evil grow progressively within. At the same time, there is also growth in self-justification. Pride and self-righteousness are worn like a necklace on display.

God becomes more and more remote, and the self is there to fill the void—ever more stable and settled in its willfulness and falsehood. A blindness ensues that covers the soul with a callousness toward God and a loss of restraint toward evil.[52]

Thus, evil can mature. From infancy it grows to adulthood. Now, more than ever, it settles in its combative role against God.

---

51 Jeremiah 17:9; Genesis 6:5.

52 Ephesians 4:17-19.

18

PATTERN RECOGNITION

"But we know that the law is good, provided one uses it legitimately. We know that the law is not meant for a righteous person, but for the lawless and rebellious, for the ungodly and sinful, for the unholy and irreverent, for those who kill their fathers and mothers, for murderers, for the sexually immoral and males who have sex with males, for slave traders, liars, perjurers, and for whatever else is contrary to the sound teaching that conforms to the gospel concerning the glory of the blessed God, which was entrusted to me."

(1 Timothy 1:8-11)

To what do we compare evil in order to determine why it is evil? We cannot compare it to ourselves or our opinions. Evil can only be compared to that standard which God Himself reveals. That standard is God's law summarized by the Ten Commandments. They contain a summary of God's moral standards for human beings.

Angels cannot be held to those commandments, rather they are held to that moral code that underlies the commandments. For God's own being and nature is embodied in the Ten Commandments. Love to God and love to others summarizes

His law, as the statement "God is love" summarizes the holy and perfect nature of God.

To recognize evil, we must understand God revealed by God Himself. We must begin with His Word, the Bible. We use His moral code, the Ten Commandments, and compare the nature of God to all others.[53] Without such a standard, there can be no absolute definition of evil. For all behavior and thought will only become that which the dominant creature willfully expresses.

Satan desires no recognition of God's law. He would prefer his own standard for his own justification and comfort. He has no desire (indeed no ability) to conform to God's law as an act of love and devotion to God.[54] His obedience, if seen, is feigned and deceptive.

Because Satan can falsely adhere to God's laws,[55] discerning his deceptions becomes most difficult. Only God can clearly reveal Satan's lies when they are coated with righteous behavior.

Yet, most of Satan's activity is more clearly seen as directly contrary to God's law. The obvious elements of evil and sin contradict God's law, while the more subtle deceptions and lies coated in obedience to God's law require more time and care to discern.

---

53   Romans 3:19.

54   Compare with Romans 8:7-8.

55   2 Corinthians 11:14.

19

THE TEMPTATION OF POWER

"Then the tempter approached him and said, 'If you are the Son of God, tell these stones to become bread.'"

(**Matthew 4:3**)

The old adage that power corrupts and absolute power corrupts absolutely[56] is certainly true when unconstrained by a humility toward and faith in God as the true Absolute. The holy angels that are mighty in power understand this and rest contentedly upon God's sovereign greatness, without fear of being moved even slightly. No evil can reach them as they rest securely under the shelter of the Almighty.[57]

But wandering and fallen beings yield to no such constraints. They do not hide in God's goodness from temptation's power. Indeed, they themselves are a source of temptation's power. For it was the glory of their power that seems to have led them astray.

---

56   Lord Acton; https://en.wikipedia.org/wiki/John_Dalberg-Acton%2C_1st_Baron_Acton.

57   Proverbs 18:10.

Now, their power encourages their continued evil behavior. The further from God the soul moves, the fewer the constraints on evil and the greater the deception becomes of one's own glory and supposed authority.

Power can become intoxicating as others fawn and marvel at the one so seemingly glorious. Monuments have been built to the supposed glory of men. Their conceit has led them to build vast structures and filled their minds with deluded hopes of future glory and grandeur. This same intoxicating spirit lies behind the allurement and practice of pornography.

The fallen being has no means to stave off the deluding temptations of power. The promise of glory, recognition, and power becomes an idol many fallen creatures cannot resist.

Satan is an expert at filling the minds of humans with delusions of grandeur, far removed from the humble dwelling place of God's almighty hand. Success, legitimate or illegitimate, can be used by Satan to puff up pride and self-exaltation.

From such heights many a soul has fallen. And the fall is always harder than the rise. History is replete with examples.

20

CHAOS

"For where there is envy and selfish ambition, there is disorder and every evil practice."

(James 3:16)

Chaos is never good. Contrary to what some perceive, chaos is the devil's tool to disrupt and reorganize to accomplish his will. He knows the creaturely limitations that plague all finite beings and can prey on that weakness through chaos.

God does not create chaos, nor is chaos a true concept of God. Order never ceases in God's universe. Chaos becomes the lack of wisdom and understanding of the creature, never the Creator. No amount of apparent disorder is random or unknown to God. Chaos is a fabrication of evil. It is used by forces rebelling against God. And chaos exposes the limitation of finite creatures when applied to the complexities of God's universe.

God knows and understands all things. Chaos never confronts or confuses Him. The idea of chaos reveals the limitations of our understanding as finite creatures.

Chaos should be met by the believer with humble faith and trust in God. Yet, it is often the tool to produce disruption and violence. Faith and patience that rest in knowing God and His awesome wisdom and power are not found when the fallen nature goes its own way with chaos.

Satan knows how to use chaos as a raging storm, which has the potential to bring destruction or a shift in power. Chaos feeds on ignorance, discontent, malice, and anger. Satan is, therefore, well qualified to provoke it. Sadly, the fallen human condition is also vulnerable to its tactics and its consequences.

God alone combats chaos as the One who rules and governs over all. No amount of apparent chaos can thwart His plans or will.[58]

That fact doesn't stop Satan from using chaos as a means of corruption and disruption to work out his will.

---

58   Compare Proverbs 19:21.

21

FIERY ARROWS

"In every situation take up the shield of faith with which you can extinguish all the flaming arrows of the evil one."

(Ephesians 6:16)

Falsehood and lies are fiery arrows that bring pain and suffering. Satan's skill at this metaphorical archery is well known. Doubts, guilt, accusations, and so on, are arrows in his quiver.

Many a soul has been wounded by a constant barrage of slander and lies. It wears down strong people and weakens their resolve to go on. How sad to see those complicit with this method of Satan.

How many political leaders have used Satan's fiery arrows to disarm and defeat their opponents so their will can reign supreme! Fiery arrows are a means of asserting the will and dominating others.

Beings whose power and pride have lifted their egos to great heights resort to fiery arrows in order to be victorious. Such tactics are often used in the political arena. The passions of sin are inflamed when power is at stake. If it's true for mankind, we can be sure it's true with fallen angels as well.

A well-placed lie. A timely bit of slander. A false accusation. An angry response. On it goes.[59] Arrows fly, and weaker souls take cover. Then the will of the archer dominates. He has taken the battlefield and proudly displays himself.

Satan is an expert at this. He knows the best arrow to do the job, and he can strike with fervency and intensity.

Without God's protective spiritual armor,[60] humans are extremely vulnerable. How many have sided with Satan merely to end the barrage? How many have given up and given in just to feel the temporary and deceitful sense of peace that comes from joining God's enemy? How often have people compromised truth and godly convictions as an attempt to stave off these arrows?

---

59 Proverbs 16:27.

60 See Ephesians 6 for a description of the Armor of God.

22

DIRECT ASSAULT

"Be sober-minded, be alert. Your adversary the devil is prowling around like a roaring lion, looking for anyone he can devour."

(1 Peter 5:8)

Many do not take seriously the fact that Satan directly assaults people. However, such assaults have been witnessed by people all over the world. They are also attested to by the Holy Scriptures. Demon possession, crippling bondage, and various other forms of assaults are real.[61]

The presence of evil beings can be sometimes felt and discerned. At other times, it is a veiled and deceptive presence, the fruit of which may take time to become evident. Nevertheless, such assaults can be overwhelming upon their victims.

Perhaps the two greatest examples of victims of direct assault by Satan are found in the Bible. They are Job, and of course, Jesus Christ. They were dramatically assaulted by Satan—and not just personally—even those around them were affected.

---

61 Many examples are found in the Gospels. E.g. Luke 13:16.

Direct assault may be indirect in that it attacks those near the one to whom Satan's malice is intended. Friends and family members can experience direct assault as an indirect way of causing grief for another.

Nightmares, near death experiences, and even blunt assaults can be directed at those near the intended victim or at the victim himself. People unaware of Satan's techniques fail to perceive his indirect assaults. Yet, their experience of assault can drive them into a kind of reserved spirit that is less likely to be fervently supportive of the one Satan is truly seeking to assault.

The victim of indirect assault may even blame the intended victim by associating their suffering with them in some way. Thus, they seal Satan's victory by moving from their former convictions and weakening the intended victim.

Those who deny the existence of demonic beings are the most susceptible to demonic assault. They completely fail to understand what is happening and find cause for it in the wrong place, thus yielding to Satan's tactic.

23

MIND GAMES

"...So that we may not be taken advantage of by Satan. For we are not ignorant of his schemes."

(2 Corinthians 2:11)

The extent to which fallen angelic creatures can read the human mind is unknown. Can they listen to our thought life? Or do they piece together our thoughts from our words? But then why would it matter that we speak, since sound waves do not appear to be the manner with which they hear?

Whatever the truth is about their ability to read the human mind, it is likely they know more about us than we can guess. They know our weaknesses, desires, fears, sins, and the things that tempt us most. They are not omniscient nor omnipresent, so we can guess their knowledge is limited as well.

However, it is beyond doubt that they can inject thoughts and make suggestions to the human mind. Doubts, fears, false guilt, and lies can manifest out of thin air. Satan may use means to make harmful accusations or suggestions, such as other people. But those harmful thoughts to the mind come directly from satanic beings.

Satan can directly possess his victims. Of course, only those not under the influence of God the Holy Spirit can be possessed by demonic spirits.[62] Once possessed, the extent of Satan's influence is not fully understood.

However, once possessed by evil spirits, it appears possible for the human to lose control and be dominated by that spirit.[63] Words and actions seem to come from another source than the human himself. Such possession may be temporary, as Satan moves about seeking to work his will.

Sadly, the fallen human spirit, devoid of the Holy Spirit, is often a willing participant to Satan's grievous suggestions. Who knows what corruption has been spawned by minds directly influenced by Satan?

We can be sure of this: Satan's goal is always to deceive, distract, and ultimately destroy people, turning people away from true devotion to Jesus Christ, while working his will through them.

---

62 1 John 4:4.

63 See Mark 5:1-20 for an example of this.

24

FALSE PROMISES

"Again, the devil took him to a very high mountain and showed him all the kingdoms of the world and their splendor. And he said to him, 'I will give you all these things if you will fall down and worship me.'"

(Matthew 4:8-9)

Perhaps one of Satan's greatest tools in seeking to manipulate people for his own purposes is his use of false promises. One need only think of the many utopian ideas in the world that convince people that they will solve the issues of peace and harmony without the need for God.

Yet, more subtle are the individualistic promises of Satan, whereby a person is led to believe he or she will attain some great gain in life, once again, without God. Such false promises deceive the intelligent as surely as they deceive the simple.[64]

Satan knows that people have a propensity to personal safety and personal gain. If he can promise one or both of those things, then he potentially has a willing pawn to carry out his will. People unwittingly do the will of Satan when they follow his false promises.

---

64 Proverbs 16:25.

False promises never materialize as expressed. Yet, the damage is usually done by gripping the minds of the unsuspecting with such promises. Once favorably aligned to a false promise, it seldom matters if the promise is fulfilled. The victim can be further manipulated and strung along by other false promises.

Unfortunately, sometimes those false promises come wrapped in spiritual language. They appear to be "from God," when all along they are really Satan's lies to puff up the victims and lead them down a road that distracts them from humble, faithful service to God.[65]

More dramatically, however, is the way Satan leads masses of people to a false utopian mindset through political revolution and upheaval. Countless people have died in the hysteria Satan produces by elevating philosophical ideas, devoid of God, to a place of prominence. By these ideas, or "ideals," people hope to find that silver bullet—the pure way that leads to peace and harmony. However, God is nowhere in their mind, and little do they realize, their last state will be worse than their first.

False promises also show up in politics. Satan finds many willing pawns by promising them greatness in exchange for their unwitting devotion to him.

---

65   Religious fervor has been known to lead people to break God's laws while thinking they are serving God. See John 16:2.

25

CLOAKING

"And no wonder! For Satan disguises himself as an angel of light."

(2 Corinthians 11:14)

To cloak something is to cover it or hide it. Satan knows how to cloak evil ideas and plans in issues that seem good or just. If people believe their cause to be just, they won't fully think through the means they use or the consequences their ideas and actions might have.

This scheme of Satan is often used in the political realm. Actions and ideas are promoted that cover a more sinister scheme of diverting people away from God's will and toward Satan's own will. People are led by the emotions of the moment or by the confidence that "if they don't do it, their opponent will," to actions they'd otherwise consider wrong.

Emotion can become a powerful ally of Satan. He was able to make Eve act emotionally by disobeying God and trusting her feelings more than God's command. Satan knows that humans will trade common sense for good feelings. He knows he can lead people into irrational, and otherwise inappropriate, actions once he has convinced them to act by their feelings.

Satan is also skilled at creating a false sense of justice in people through lies. He convinces them that their supposed opponent is going to lie or doesn't care about true justice—convincing them to lie and act unjustly. Then they do so with a spirit of self-justification and "righteous" fervor that is really a lie.

This technique of cloaking turns otherwise ordinary and calm people into pawns of Satan's plans. Because they act by emotion or upon a falsehood, they are unwitting allies of rebellion against God.

Sadly, Satan can also cloak his plans in religious fervor and zeal. All kinds of religions, including Christianity, can become the cloaking method of Satan. How much religious hypocrisy has gone unnoticed by Satan's victims?

26

THE DECEPTION OF AUTONOMY

"In fact, God knows that when you eat it your eyes will be opened and you will be like God, knowing good and evil."

(Genesis 3:5)

When Satan tempted Eve in the Garden of Eden with the idea that she would be like God, with the knowledge of good and evil, it was the deception of a promise of autonomy. Autonomy is self-governance without reference to God. It is an ancient temptation and one that results in direct rebellion against God, ultimately leaving Satan "pulling the strings."

God never intended the human will to function *absolutely* autonomously. As with all His creatures, He made us to function within the boundaries He created for us. Unlike animal life, human and angelic life have moral boundaries they are required to function within, and those boundaries agree with God's character and righteousness, referred to as God's Law.

Within the boundaries of God's Law, angels and people are free to exercise choices. Within those boundaries are true love, peace, and liberty. God created us to live under His authority as our boundary, not absolutely autonomously.

But Satan tempts people to break those boundaries, to see them as God's restrictions to their freedom.[66] Satan tempts humans to promote their own will as their highest goal. And he deludes them into thinking that their collective will is better than God's.

Yet, as history shows and as the Bible teaches, when people act autonomously without a true reference to God, it results in chaos and rebellion. It always ends up focusing on the will of one person over others.[67] The battle of wills always degenerates into some form of dictatorship, where the strongest will prevails.

Ironically, autonomy can also appear in a religious form, when humility is replaced by a pride in one's own views.

God intended us to act under His authority, always seeking His will. That requires faith, humility, patience, and the Holy Spirit—all of which Satan vehemently opposes by his deception of autonomy.

---

66   See Psalm 2.

67   Saul's disobedience is an example. See 1 Samuel 15:22-23.

27

VIOLENCE AS A MEANS TO AN END

"Now the earth was corrupt in God's sight, and the earth was filled with wickedness."

(Genesis 6:11)

When Satan cannot get his own way through deception, he resorts to violent means. It is a mystery how he uses his powers among angelic beings, but we know he fights to get his own way.[68] He is surely master among his own fallen angels, by virtue of his superior power. God made Satan a mighty angel.[69] Yet, as discussed previously, that might and the glory likely contributed to Satan's downfall.

With humans, Satan is skilled at inciting violence. He knows how to stir up human pride. He is skilled at setting up standoffs between camps of differing views and then turning their frustration and impatience into seemingly justifiable violence.

The line between justifiable and unjustifiable violence is blurred by Satan. One may argue for a "just war" based on clear

---

68 See Revelation 12 and Satan's battle with Michael.

69 Examples of Satan's power are seen throughout Scripture.

violations of human rights, whereby one's freedom to act under God and in good conscience is hindered. Some would call this self-defense. But there is a great temptation to elevate our opinions to such a height that violence becomes justifiable when truly it is not.

Satan is a master at deceiving people into thinking their cause is just, or even divine in origin, thus making violence justifiable. He also convinces people that if they don't act now that the other side will. He feeds impatience and pride. Young adults are especially susceptible to this tactic, as are dictators and those vainly deluded by power.

How many wars and revolutions has Satan fueled? How many men have died? How many families have lost loved ones? How many widows and orphans has he produced? And how many innocent bystanders have been killed in the fury of violence?

Will we never wake up to Satan's lies about the use of violence? Will we continue to allow his deceptions to blind us into foolish action?[70]

---

70 Proverbs 16:29.

28

EVIL ALLIANCES

*"When a person's ways please the Lord,
he makes even his enemies to be at peace with him."*

(Proverbs 16:7)

It's interesting to see how evil allies itself with evil for evil purposes. The alliance is not for peace but for purpose—the purpose of dominance. Therefore, the ruse is that one evil is planning to take over the other and be dominant. It works like this: A allies with B to defeat C, but the real goal of A is to defeat B as well and become dominant.

This tactic arises from the unprincipled nature of evil. It has no compunction about who it befriends as long as its ultimate goals can be achieved. This alliance strategy is a divide-and-conquer technique that shocks its opponents by overwhelming their defenses and abilities.

Satan is also a master at this divide and conquer. He has even attempted it in the Church. His strategy is to overwhelm orthodoxy—to confuse it, break down its defenses, and overwhelm its ability to respond.

God has always rescued His truth by the power of the Holy Spirit. But that fact does not dissuade Satan. He continues to pursue after godly theology with a ruthless spirit to destroy it.

Satan's strategy of insincere alliances to divide and conquer are also seen among nations and philosophical groups. Temporary victory drives the human spirit on with pride and a sense of indestructability. The long-term consequences of their actions are seldom weighed against the apparent glory to be achieved by dominating another.

One wonders about the pleasure or satisfaction Satan takes in watching people destroy each other. In that mayhem, he knows he has a good chance of weakening the cause of Christ and delaying his own inevitable doom by hindering the spread of the gospel of Christ.

But God is also at work in His world! The Lord will never be outsmarted or outdone by His creatures. He can take their worst behavior and turn it against them.[71]

---

71   Colossians 2:15. The Lord triumphed over Satan through the cross.

29

DECEITFUL MANIPULATIONS

*"Then these men said,
'We will never find any charge against this Daniel
unless we find something against him concerning the law of his God.'"*

(Daniel 6:5)

There is no end to the deceitfulness of a fallen being bent on asserting its will over others. A conniving, scheming attitude results from a fundamental malcontent. That malcontent is especially worked up when those they disagree with are seemingly standing in the way of their will.

The evidence for deceitful manipulation is plentiful in the Bible, as it is seen in human discord. To name a few examples: how the enemies of Daniel tried to destroy him by creating a law they knew he would disobey because of his faith in God; how Haman did something similar to destroy all the Jews during the time of Queen Esther; or how the pagan people of the land tried to hinder the rebuilding of the Jerusalem Temple and walls in the post-exilic times.

From these human examples, we deduce satanic influence. The malice demonstrated rises to the level of spiritual persecution, which surely points to the devil as the key orchestrator. The main reason for this deduction is the persecution is leveled at those in a covenant relationship with God. That fact points us to something more than just human malice.[72]

We learn from this that Satan's tactics can become very political and very intermeshed with human events.[73] His tactic is to confuse, destroy, hinder, and entangle people in webs of fear and confusion so they cease their current pursuits or become consumed in a defensive posture.

Such tactics arise from the lawless nature of evil. It acts without love or mercy. It has a self-serving code of conduct. It is self-righteous in its deceit. Yet sadly, it is also quite blind to the harshness and brutality of its ways, carrying on blithely while it destroys others.

Perhaps saddest of all, is that this deceit has been seen in some religious figures in the Church throughout Christian history. One wonders how the devil gets into the Church, but he obviously uses sinful human nature to do it. Once there, the devil seeks to destroy from within, by undermining truth and displacing or neutralizing godly people.

---

72 Refer to Zechariah 3:1-2. Satan is clearly seen as a key figure in opposition to the rebuilding of Jerusalem after the Babylonian Exile.

73 Satan's intermeshing with human events it very apparent in the prophecies of Daniel chapters 10-11, for example.

30

SATAN'S GOAL

"You said to yourself, 'I will ascend to the heavens; I will set up my throne above the stars of God. I will sit on the mount of the gods' assembly, in the remotest parts of the North.'"

(Isaiah 14:13)

The goal of all fallen creatures is to replace God's will with their own will and God's glory with their own glory. Satan is especially focused on that goal as a means of self-justification and a vengeful reaction to God's rejection of his pride.[74]

All fallen creatures are susceptible to that same goal. And Satan is skilled at artfully manipulating vain people to accomplish his goals. How many world leaders have fallen victim to his false promises of glory and supposed immortality?

Never doubt Satan's ability to manipulate humans to accomplish his own goals. Governments are a primary target. But

---

74 This conclusion is derived from the nature of pride and its unwillingness to admit wrong. See also Proverbs 16:18. And, note how pride deceives people in Jeremiah 49:16 and Obadiah 1:3.

all aspects of leadership can be targets, from families to companies. Take down a leader and many others are adversely affected. Take possession of a leader's goals so he accomplishes your own, and you have a willing, albeit unwitting, comrade.

All Satan's efforts focus on steering people away from a sincere and genuine devotion to God through faith in His Son, Jesus Christ. Satan has made himself God's rival and has attempted to take the glory and honor due only to God's Son. We should never doubt that all Satan does is calculated to exalt himself, while replacing God in the hearts and minds of people.

Nations too, given the fallen nature of people, are easily steered into the same directions as Satan's goals. Only God's divine intervention or His Spirit's influence can foil Satan's goals among the nations.

One must believe in the power of prayer and devotion to God, along with the proclamation of the gospel, as the only true weapons to thwart Satan's influence among the nations.[75] Prayer and faith force Satan out into the open, exposing his limitations. Then, he will melt away and wait, biding his time as he scours for another opportunity.[76]

Vigilance in faith and prayer can keep evil at bay. By faith and prayer, we refuse to be willing participants in Satan's evil goals, and we keep God's glory alone in focus.

---

[75] See also James 4:7-8.

[76] Luke 4:13.

31

SATAN'S IMPACT

"But Pharaoh responded,
'Who is the Lord that I should obey him by letting Israel go?
I don't know the Lord, and besides, I will not let Israel go.'"

(Exodus 5:2)

Satan has had a profound impact on humanity. He is directly responsible for the fall of Eve, followed by Adam. He has brought a curse upon the world, and the result has been a great deal of violence and harm. Also, he obscures God's glory revealed in all of creation.[77]

However, there is one individual in the Bible that helps us understand the full impact of Satan on people—the Pharaoh of Egypt during the time of Moses. The Israelites had become enslaved in Egypt, and God raised up Moses to deliver them from this bondage.

God prepared Moses by humbling him in exile from Egypt and then revealing Himself to him on Mount Sinai. There, God

---

[77] Contrast how the holy angels see God's glory in creation in Isaiah 6:3.

called Moses to go and stand before Pharaoh and demand he let the Israelites go free. Moses went before Pharaoh and conveyed God's message.

Pharaoh's response to Moses is recorded in Exodus 5:2, "Who is the Lord that I should obey him by letting Israel go? I don't know the Lord, and besides, I will not let Israel go."

In Pharaoh's response we see the spirit of mankind's rebellion that is the direct result of Satan's influence. Three characteristics stand out in Pharaoh's words. He *questioned authority*, asking "Who is God?" He *doubted authority*, claiming "I don't know God." He *resisted authority*, saying "I will not obey God."

The mantra, "question, doubt, resist," is prevalent in the rebellious spirit that seeks to impose its own will on others. Sin leads people to struggle for their own way, pushing God aside, disregarding His word and wisdom, and seeking to establish their own authority.

God is, however, the one who should never be questioned because He is *always truthful*, never be doubted because He is *always faithful*, and never be resisted because He is *always just and righteous*. But sin and Satan have blinded people's hearts to choose rebellion.

Mankind is in a battle—with Satan as their leader—against God. It's a battle they cannot win. It's a battle that has eternal consequences. It's a battle people would do well to ensure they are on the side of righteousness![78]

---

78   Isaiah 55:6-7.

32

SATAN'S IMAGE

"What then? Are we any better off? Not at all! For we have already charged that both Jews and Greeks are all under sin, as it is written: There is no one righteous, not even one."

(Romans 3:9-10)

If God made man in His own image, then the fall of man has reshaped man into the image of Satan. Not that God's image is gone; that's impossible no matter how hard people try to expunge it. But Satan's image has been imprinted through sin. Sinful human nature bears the marks of Satan's image and has the marks of Satan's behavior.

Satan's image in mankind leads to a self-oriented and rebellious spirit. It is the spirit of going one's own way and of ignoring God's will.[79]

However, people often fail to see themselves as rebellious. That sets them up as opponents of God and allies of Satan, whether they see it that way or not.

---

79   Isaiah 53:6.

Sin is Satan's image. Sin is lawlessness. That is, it is contrary to God's Law and seeks to establish its own. And Satan is skilled at helping people justify their sinful behavior, thus urging them on to further separation from God.

So long as people are following their own desires and ignoring God's will, they are under Satan's power. He will defend them as citizens of his parasite kingdom.[80] Thus, it is often difficult and fraught with opposition from Satan when sinners begin to see the light of the gospel of Jesus.

But God is mighty and awesome. His truth will prevail, because His word is inherently powerful. As God spoke and formed the universe, so His word has the power to transform souls, delivering them from Satan's tyranny and restoring His own image in them.[81]

Therefore, it is never a vain effort to preach the gospel. The word of God is powerful, as the Spirit of God uses it to convert souls. By that same word and Spirit, sinful men and women are restored to God and His image is restored in them!

---

80   This is Christ's world (Colossians 1:16-17), and therefore Satan's rule is parasitic in nature.

81   See 2 Corinthians 4:6, 5:17, and Colossians 1:13-14.

33

THE DEVIL MADE ME DO IT

*"For all have sinned
and fall short of the glory of God."*

(Romans 3:23)

"The devil made me do it." No, he did not! People act according to their own will and desires.[82] All creatures God made that are subject to His moral boundaries are also responsible to God and will be held accountable for their choices. No one will be able to claim an exemption from God's judgments on the basis that Satan made them do it. If they "did it," then they will be held accountable by God.[83]

This aspect of reality—accountability to God—shows us the callousness and cruelty of Satan. He knows full well how God will judge people's actions. Yet, he continues to lead people astray with total disregard for their soul.

---

[82] James 1:13-15.

[83] Revelation 20:11-15; Romans 3:19.

The fact of Satan's callousness or disregard for the souls of others is often revealed in people. History is filled with examples of leaders who led their fellow man down paths of rebellion against God, without regard for their eternal good. In fact, a false promise of eternal good is often a means to get people to risk their lives. The deception of immortality becomes a powerful motivator to make people do things that, ironically, defy God's Law.

God is the ultimate Judge. Satan cunningly deceives human hearts into breaking God's laws, thus incurring God's judgment. True, the human heart is fallen and doesn't need Satan's "push" to get it to do wrong. But he knows just how to "push" sinners in the wrong direction.

Let this be a sober warning to all who read this: God will hold us all accountable for our actions.

There will be no excuses on the Day of Judgment. The only way out of condemnation is God's way, through the means He Himself has designed, provided, and accomplished. Through Jesus Christ, God has accomplished the forgiveness of sins we need in order to stand without condemnation on Judgment Day.

34

BLAME IT ON THE DEVIL

"For we must all appear before the judgment seat of Christ, so that each may be repaid for what he has done in the body, whether good or evil."

(2 Corinthians 5:10)

Is Satan to blame for all the evil in the world today? No. People are responsible for much of the evil in our society, because we are fallen creatures. But is Satan behind a great deal of evil? Does Satan motivate and direct evil intents using sinful hearts? Yes.

Sadly, many people reject Satan as a source of evil because they don't see him, nor do they recognize his presence or influences. They think of Satan as a caricature. Only God Himself knows the full extent of Satan's culpability and involvement, but we should never discount him.

Satan's schemes are behind many of the institutionalized anti-Christian spirits in the world. Indeed, Satan is the spirit of anti-Christ.[84] He is the spirit behind all that opposes the rule of Christ in people's hearts. True, the human heart is innately dead in sin,

---

84   2 Thessalonians 2:1-12.

but anti-Christian sentiment has a distinctive satanic influence in it that seems to transcend the basic sin and pride of the human heart.

The Bible predicts the coming of an evil and lawless one, whose activity is in accordance with Satan. That anti-Christ spirit will bring its persecution of the true Church to new and unprecedented heights, unleashing on the Church the full battery of Satan's deceptions and malice. Who will be behind this anti-Christ? Satan.[85]

Men and women are capable of great sins. Fallen human nature is inherently rebellious and disobedient to God. People account for much of the evil in the world, but we can never underestimate Satan's influence.

Sadly, many people see evil and reject God rather than blame Satan. What a mistake! God does no evil, and such a thought is horrible. He is always worthy of our love and trust.

Satan, on the other hand, is a liar and a murderer. He is never trustworthy. He is a tyrant bent on malice toward God. Do you see evil? Don't count out the devil.

---

85 Revelation 13.

PART III
GOD'S RESPONSE TO EVIL

We now begin to think through how the Bible describes God's solution to the problem of evil. God will be victorious over evil. How? What did He do? What does His wise and amazing plan look like?

THOUGHTS ON THE ORIGIN AND EVOLUTION OF EVIL

35

SEEING AS GOD SEES

"For we don't dare classify or compare ourselves with some who commend themselves. But in measuring themselves by themselves and comparing themselves to themselves, they lack understanding."

(2 Corinthians 10:12)

People tend to compare themselves within their own historical situation. They tend to see themselves in the context of their culture and times. Therefore, they compare themselves with themselves. And they justify themselves on the basis of their own estimations. But that's not how God sees people, or angels for that matter.[86]

God compares His creatures to His Law. On Judgement Day, it won't be how heroic, dynamic, assertive, important, successful, or whatever a person is that will commend them to God.[87] The standards by which people think a person to be honorable or noble are not God's standards. God knows people far more deeply.[88]

---

86   Proverbs 14:12.

87   Jeremiah 9:23-24.

88   1 Samuel 16:7; Romans 2:12-16.

Sin and Satan blind people to the true nature of their own heart. They fail to see its wickedness, pride, lust, greed—you name it. But God sees in a way we don't. Hence, Judgment Day will be a revealing of the hearts and motives of people—and they will be without excuse.

Don't underestimate the precision and justice of God's judgments. Comparison to Him will yield an indisputable picture of the nature of each person who ever lived. His Law will be like a bright beam of light that clearly reveals the presence of sin in a person—clearly highlighting rebellion and selfishness.

The questions to ask one's self are: How do I measure up to God's Law? Do I love God? Do I serve idols? Do I ignore or abuse His name and Person? Do I sin against any of His moral laws?

The light of God's Law judges the conscience of each human being. And on Judgement Day, if a person were to stand before God on the basis of their own righteousness, that light will surely convict them that they have fallen short and deserve condemnation.

Satan does all he can to keep people blind to their condition.[89] He frustrates the spread of the gospel, deceives people, and defends his tyrannical dominance over them. He fans their vanity to think more highly of themselves than is warranted, thus inducing a false confidence to continue in their sins.

However, it is vitally important for people to understand how God sees them. Who wants to stand before the living God totally unprepared to face His assessment of them? The Bible speaks of the terrors that will come upon people unprepared to face their Maker.[90] Therefore, only a right assessment of themselves can possibly help them see the way God has provided them to escape judgment through Jesus Christ.

---

89 2 Corinthians 4:4.

90 Hebrews 10:26-27; Revelation 6:15-17.

36

RECOVERING REALITY

"Humble yourselves, therefore, under the mighty hand of God, so that he may exalt you at the proper time, casting all your cares on him, because he cares about you."

(1 Peter 5:6-7)

The earth belongs to the Lord God who made it. We humans and all angelic or heavenly beings—indeed all creation—belong to God. Reality is therefore His to define as He created it. We cannot simply go our own way and think God doesn't care.

Satan fell from the humble state of glory God gave him. As this analysis proposes, he felt the power of his own glory and failed to defer to God, wait upon God, trust in God, and seek God's will. He slowly gave precedence to his own will. He allowed a presumptuous and false view of reality that exalted his own authority to overcome him. In that spirit, he abused God's authority by rebelling against Him and pushing his own dominance.

The angels that joined Satan were led astray by Satan's false reality. They too became deceived into trusting themselves over God. The spirit of a humble servant under God's authority, loving

God and others as their self, departed from their consciousness. They became focused solely on themselves. Ironically, instead of being servants of God, they became slaves of Satan, while Satan became a slave to his own pride.

Translate the above to mankind. What is true of fallen angels is sadly true of fallen humanity as well. We have lost the spirit of love and devotion to God as His humble servants who seek His will, wait upon Him, trust in Him, and obey Him.

The result is a kind of chaos that Satan uses to work his will. The result is rebellion against God. The result is that one generation after another continues in its own way, feeling autonomous.

To recover from this state, human beings must repent, turn from their present course of life, and trust in God's way. To recover true reality, we must change. God has no reason or need to change. Ours is the insult. Ours must be the change.[91]

Satan does all he can to prevent that change.

---

91 Isaiah 45:22; Mark 1:15; Acts 17:30-31.

37

DIVINE REMEDY

*"For God loved the world in this way:
He gave his one and only Son, so that everyone who believes in him
will not perish but have eternal life."*

(John 3:16)

Humans are no match for fallen angels. Whatever the powers of fallen angels, they are far greater than ours. They are immortal and cannot die. Our physical weapons have no effect on them. Only faith, true faith in the name of Jesus, has victory over them.

God will honor His Son's name, and Satan knows it. But something more is required for human beings to escape the consequences of our fallen nature. Only God can do for us what we cannot do for ourselves. Only God's remedy will work to heal us and restore us to a right relationship with Him.

God's remedy is revealed as His grace. God gives to us not what we deserve, which is His just wrath, but what we do not deserve. God forgives our sins, makes us right with Himself, upholds us, and then brings us to His glorious presence one day. That is salvation, deliverance, redemption, and reconciliation.

God's remedy restores us to a right understanding of our place as His creatures. That understanding gets darkened by our fallen nature. But the light of God's grace illuminates and transforms our minds to rightly see ourselves as humble creatures who, at best, merely reflect the smallest rays of God's awesome glory.

God will not give His glory to another. The Father, Son, and Holy Spirit are one glorious God—deserving and worthy of all praise, honor, and glory. Our purpose in life is to grow through the knowledge of God in Jesus Christ so that we can better reflect His true glory by our thoughts, words, and deeds.

The means God used to redeem fallen sinners is the death of His Son on the cross. Upon that cross, God buried the arrows of divine justice in His own Son so that we do not have to bear them.

Turning from sin and to Christ by faith is how we can receive God's grace accomplished through the cross. That grace is confirmed to us by the fact that Jesus rose from the dead. Death, the penalty of our sins, could not hold down God's Son, who rose victoriously and defeated it.

And by the death and resurrection of Christ, God destroyed both the curse of sin, which is death, and crushed Satan. Yes, Satan is now a completely defeated foe. So much so, that the Bible records the holy angels drove him out of heaven for eternity after Christ's victory over death on the cross.[92]

No longer will the holy angels tolerate Satan's falsehood in heaven. No more will Satan have an audience with God to make accusations against His people. The holy angels understand the whole picture now and will defend heaven itself at any cost.

Those glorious angels will one day return, following their infinitely glorious Leader, Jesus Christ. They had known the Son before His humble earthly ministry. But now they know the full

---

92   Revelation 12:7-10.

story of what it took for God to redeem fallen humans, and they are amazed by God's grace.[93]

In fact, holy angels rejoice when sinners repent and turn to Jesus. They know what God's wrath looks like, and they know the consequences of rejecting Him. So too, they know the depths it cost God to redeem. Therefore, their joy is great when human beings are returned to a right relationship with God.[94]

What an amazing thing is God's grace! To see fallen sinners restored must be a marvelous sight to the eyes of holy angels. Is it any wonder they are eager to aid those who have come to Jesus for salvation?[95]

God's goals are clear and will prevail. He is going to defeat and remove from His direct presence all that offends His glory.[96] Satan and the fallen angels' days are numbered. Alas, so are the days of all people who reject Christ. Fallen angels are fixed in their state. But we sinners can repent, believe, and receive God's gift of salvation through Jesus, His Son.

What will you do? Will you continue the futile course of life under Satan's influence? Or will you surrender? Will you admit defeat? You cannot defeat God. You cannot assert your will over His. You cannot justify or save yourself. You cannot earn salvation.

Grace, God's grace, that's what we need. And it is freely received through Jesus Christ. Abandon the allegiance with evil and fallen nature and humbly look to Jesus. Restore your human nature to its proper place—under God's authority. Be a humble servant of God, with the goal to reflect His glory so that in all things God has the preeminence He deserves. To Him be all the glory!

---

93   1 Peter 1:12.

94   Luke 15:1-10.

95   Hebrews 1:14; 13:2.

96   Revelation 21:27.

THOUGHTS ON THE ORIGIN AND EVOLUTION OF EVIL

38

GOD'S TRIUMPH

*"Then I heard a loud voice in heaven say,
'The salvation and the power and the kingdom of our God
and the authority of his Christ have now come, because the accuser of
our brothers and sisters, who accuses them before our God
day and night, has been thrown down.'"*

(Revelation 12:10)

Creation is God's wisdom and power, gentleness and love, and majesty and glory, on vivid display. He is redeeming it from the fall of angels and human beings. He is going to restore it to the glory and righteousness He intended when creation began.[97]

All that offends God's glory, be it angels or people, He will remove from His glorious presence one day. That is hell. Hell is the place where the rebellious and disobedient will one day be finally banished from God's glory. Their offense will one day be completely removed.[98] And with their removal, God will establish

---

97   Revelation 21:1.

98   Revelation 20:11-15.

a new order, where stability and righteousness will reign on into eternity.[99]

To do this, God triumphed over sin and Satan by the weakness of humanity. Through the frailty of the incarnation of His Son, God destroyed the arrogance and rebellion of those against Him. Satan's love of self-glory became his own undoing, as he lifted the Son of God onto the cross through the hands of wicked men. There Jesus died, not for Himself, but for the sins of human beings. There, Jesus destroyed and crushed the devil by the devil's own hand. Satan's selfishness and malice became his own undoing and became the tool in God's hand to work salvation.

God is triumphant. Nothing and no one will displace His glory. What a futile effort it is for anyone, human or angelic, to try.

God is the true Champion of His own universe. Who is on His side? Who will join His family of loyal sons and daughters as servants of Jesus Christ?

Christians receive a glory not our own that shines from God through Jesus Christ. We receive the blessings of God's inheritance from His one and only Son, Jesus Christ. God reserves places of honor for redeemed sinners to reveal His grace and love and to shame the rebellious who seek their own glory above His.

God is triumphant. His will be done on earth as it is in heaven.

---

99   Revelation 21:3-4.

39

GOD'S HEART

*"The Lord is gracious and compassionate,
slow to anger and great in faithful love.
The Lord is good to everyone;
his compassion rests on all he has made."*

(Psalm 145:8-9)

I am convinced that God's heart is grieved over the state of fallen creatures. He takes no delight in their destruction.[100] God is not unmoved by their fall, in the sense of His emotion toward them as we can understand God's emotion.

God is not perturbed by events in the way that we are. He knows all things. Yet, His love means He is moved by the plight of His creatures. He even loves His enemies, as evidenced by His patience and kindness to them. He has even shown patience to Satan.

God always acts in accordance with His perfect and holy nature. He is not moved to change Himself or His plans, because they are always perfect, and His will is always best. His steady hand

---

100   Ezekiel 18:23.

of Providence continues to supply all life with what it needs to exist, even while fallen creatures rebel against Him.

So, one is led to ask: Why continue in rebellion against God? What purpose can it serve to try to force your will above His? We cannot prevail against God. And why reject so loving a heart as God has? Why test Him to see if His wrath is real? Is your pride worth the loss of your soul? Is repentance and faith so unreasonable for God to ask of us sinners to restore a right relationship to Him? He has done all we need for salvation by His grace through His Son.

Fallen angels have no means of redemption. That fact should forever banish from our minds the notion that God will not really execute His wrath. He will. To continue to reject His heart of compassion and mercy through Jesus Christ is to doom yourself to that wrath.[101]

But what joy and delight there will be as the redeemed of the Lord, through Jesus their Savior, join the holy angels to worship Him! God the Father, Son, and Holy Spirit will be praised, honored, and adored by all who love Him. Will you be there among that group?[102]

---

101   Revelation 21:8; 22:15.

102   Revelation 22:17, "Both the Spirit and the bride say, "Come!" Let anyone who hears, say, "Come!" Let the one who is thirsty come. Let the one who desires take the water of life freely."

www.ingramcontent.com/pod-product-compliance
Lightning Source LLC
Chambersburg PA
CBHW052113110526
44592CB00013B/1592